OUR UNIVERSE

THE Solar System

BY MARION DANE BAUER

ILLUSTRATED BY JOHN WALLACE

Ready-to-Read

Simon Spotlight
New York Amsterdam/Antwerp London
Toronto Sydney/Melbourne New Delhi

For Barbara Hill,
the Sun in my world
—M. D. B.

For Eli
—J. W.

SIMON SPOTLIGHT
An imprint of Simon & Schuster Children's Publishing Division
1230 Avenue of the Americas, New York, New York 10020

This Simon Spotlight edition December 2025

For information about special discounts for bulk purchases, please contact Simon & Schuster Special Sales at 1-866-506-1949 or business@simonandschuster.com.
Simon & Schuster strongly believes in freedom of expression and stands against censorship in all its forms. For more information, visit BooksBelong.com.
The Simon & Schuster Speakers Bureau can bring authors to your live event. For more information or to book an event, contact the Simon & Schuster Speakers Bureau at 1-866-248-3049 or visit our website at www.simonspeakers.com.
Manufactured in China 0825 SDI

Glossary

✦ **asteroids** (say: A-stuh-royds): small, rocky bodies found in space.

✦ **axis** (say: AK-suss): an imaginary straight line about which a geometric body rotates.

✦ **comets** (say: KAH-mutts): space objects made of ice that often have long tails made of gas and dust.

✦ **dwarf planets** (say: DWORF PLA-nuhts): space objects that circle the Sun but do not shift other objects from their orbit.

✦ **gas giant** (say: GAS JIE-unt): a large planet composed of gas surrounding a solid core.

✦ **ice giant** (say: IESS JIE-unt): a large planet composed of icy materials surrounding a rocky core.

✦ **meteoroids** (say: MEE-tee-uh-royds): space rocks that range in size from grains to small asteroids.

✦ **objects** (say: AWB-jekts): material things that can be observed.

✦ **orbit** (say: OR-buht): to move in a circle around another object.

Note to readers: Some of these words may have more than one definition. The definitions above match how these words are used in this book.

Do you know what
is at the center of
our solar system?
Our shining Sun!

Eight planets,
several **dwarf planets**, and
over a million **asteroids**
all **orbit** the Sun.

These **objects**, along with **comets**, **meteoroids**, moons, dust, and gases, make up our solar system.

Mercury lies closest
to the Sun.

It is the smallest planet.
It is the fastest, too.
Mercury circles the Sun
every eighty-eight days.

Next comes Venus,
the hottest planet.

You can see Venus in
the sky just before sunrise
and just after sunset.

Earth is the only planet
known to support life.
Our Earth supports
every kind of life.

Giraffes and mushrooms,
butterflies and sharks,
giant redwood trees.

And us.

Mars is the last
of the rocky planets.

People have long talked about living on Mars, but the air is toxic, and it gets very, very cold.

The asteroid belt
comes next.

It is made up of dust and rocks traveling around the Sun.

Jupiter is
a **gas giant**.
More than one
thousand Earths
could fit inside
Jupiter!

Saturn, another gas giant,
is famous for its shining rings.

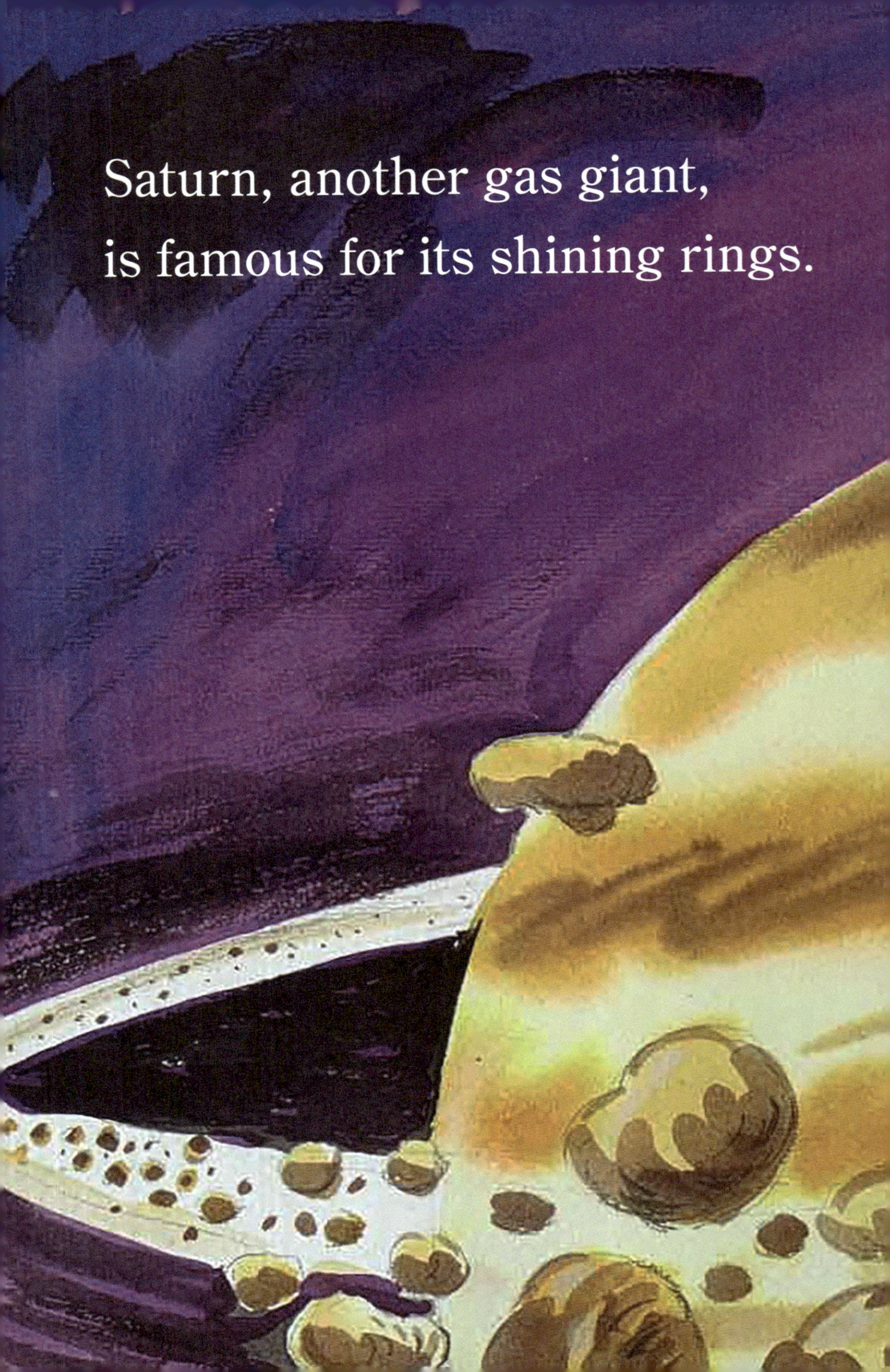

The rings are made up of ice, rocks, and dust.

Uranus is an **ice giant**.

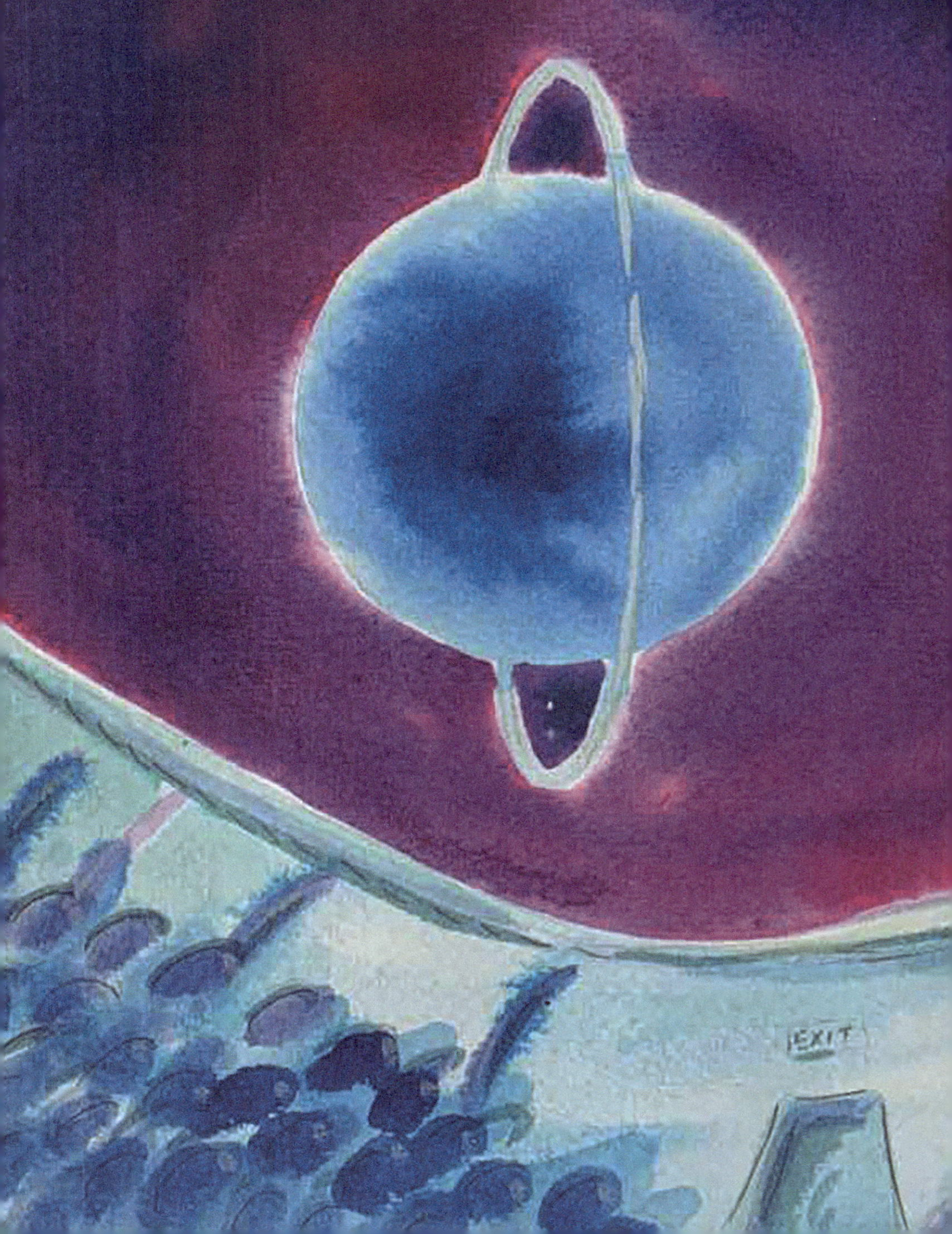

Uranus appears to spin on its side because of its tilted **axis**.

Neptune, another ice giant, is so far from the Sun that each orbit takes almost 165 Earth years.

165 Years Ago

Today

Beyond Neptune,
dwarf planets like Pluto
and hundreds of thousands
of frozen objects
circle the Sun.

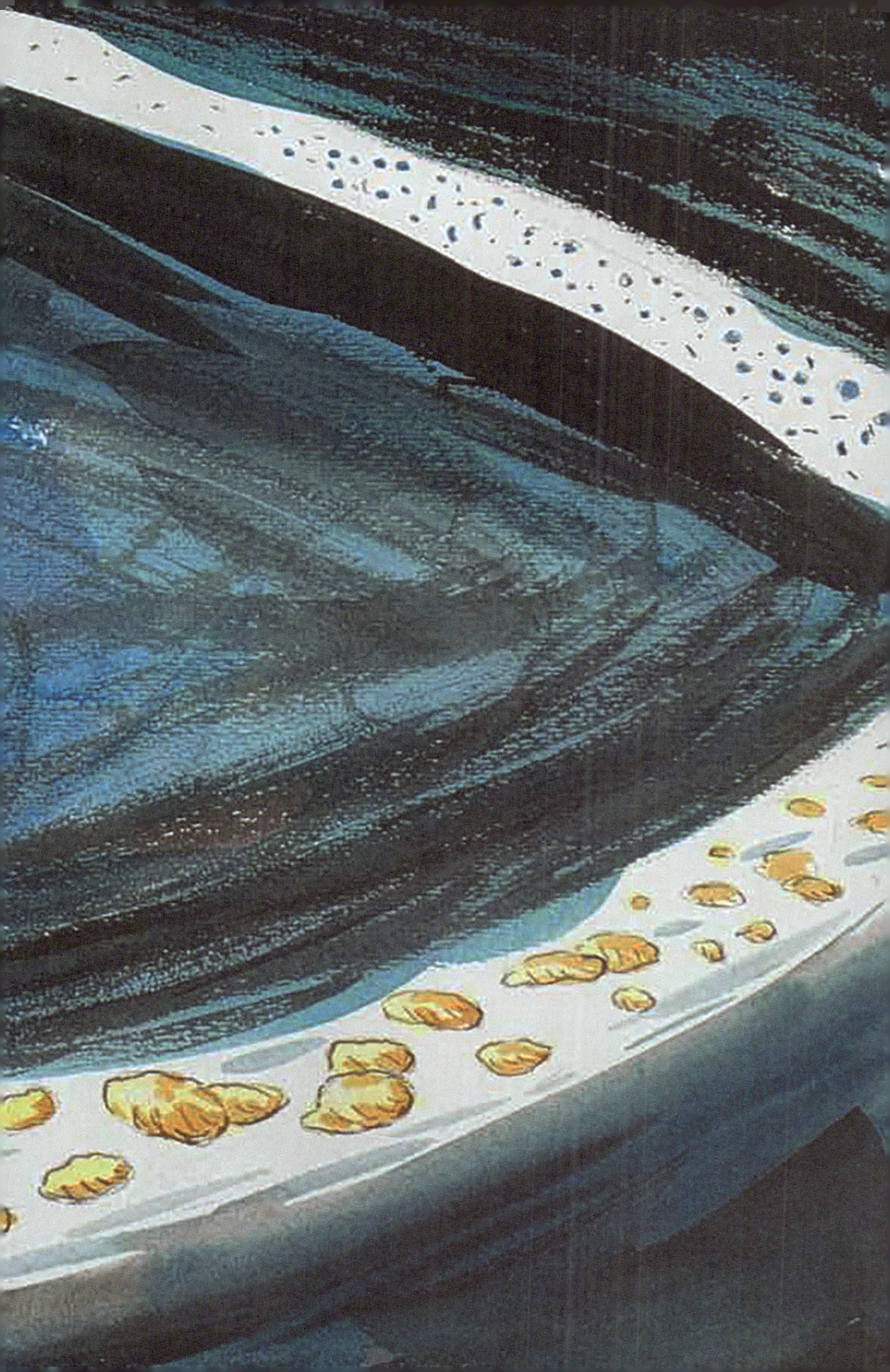

And beyond that . . .

are wonders
yet to be discovered!

Interesting Facts

- ✦ Our solar system is part of a galaxy called the Milky Way. Our Sun is one of a hundred billion stars in the Milky Way.
- ✦ Scientists classify the Sun as a yellow dwarf star.
- ✦ Gravity keeps the planets—and everything else—circling the Sun.
- ✦ The Sun is so big, more than one million Earths could fit inside it. It makes up 99.8 percent of the mass of our solar system.
- ✦ Each journey of the Earth around the Sun makes a year. Each rotation of our planet makes a day and a night.
- ✦ You could not walk on Jupiter, Saturn, Uranus, or Neptune. Their surfaces are not solid. In fact, they are made up of gases.
- ✦ Much of the time, Saturn is the most distant planet you can see without a telescope.
- ✦ Earth is in what scientists call the Goldilocks zone—not too hot, not too cold. The temperature is just right for water to be liquid.
- ✦ Scientists think that farther out than we can see, a Planet X might exist, ten times larger than Earth and about twenty times farther from the Sun than Neptune.
- ✦ Most of our solar system is empty space.

OUR UNIVERSE

Moon

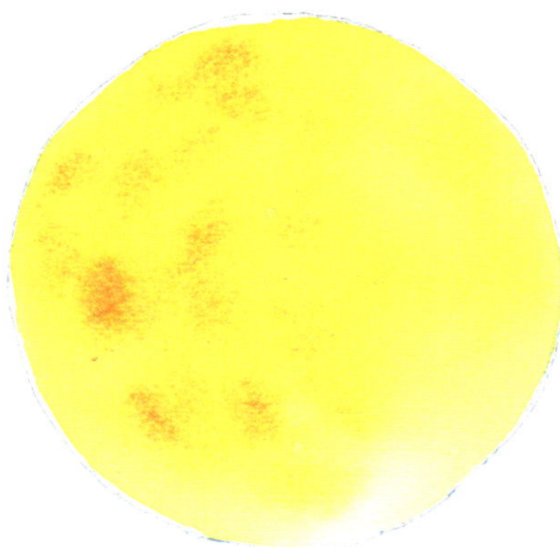

BY MARION DANE BAUER
ILLUSTRATED BY JOHN WALLACE

Ready-to-Read

Simon Spotlight
New York Amsterdam/Antwerp London
Toronto Sydney/Melbourne New Delhi

For my first grandson, Connor Dane Bauer, with love
—M. D. B.

For Zsa—J. G. W.

SIMON SPOTLIGHT
An imprint of Simon & Schuster Children's Publishing Division
1230 Avenue of the Americas, New York, New York 10020

This Simon Spotlight edition December 2025

Manufactured in China 0825 SDI

Glossary

- **asteroids** (say: A-stuh-roidz): small, rocky objects that circle the Sun just as planets do.
- **astronauts** (say: A-struh-nots): people who go into outer space. We refer to them as “cosmonauts” when they are from Russia, “spationauts” when they are from France, and “taikonauts” when they are from China.
- **eclipse** (say: ih-KLIPS): an event that happens when the Earth gets in between the Sun and the Moon so that sunlight can't reflect off the Moon.
- **gravity** (say: GRA-vuh-tee): a pulling force that works across space. The bigger an object is, the more pull it has. Since Earth is larger than the Moon, Earth pulls the Moon into orbit.
- **satellite** (say: SA-tuh-lite): an object in space that circles around a bigger object. Earth has one natural satellite, the Moon. There are many man-made satellites that circle Earth too.

Note to readers: Some of these words may have more than one definition. The definitions above match how these words are used in this book.

What is that so big and
bright in our night sky?

Our Moon, of course!

Scientists are not certain how our Moon came to be.

Many think a large object slammed into our young Earth billions of years ago.

The impact sent rocks and dust flying.

In time the rocks and dust gathered to form our Moon.

The Moon is Earth's only natural **satellite**.

It travels around Earth
once every twenty-eight days.

As it travels, the Moon's
gravity pulls on our oceans.

That pull causes
low and high tides.

Our Moon lights up our night sky, but it has no light of its own.

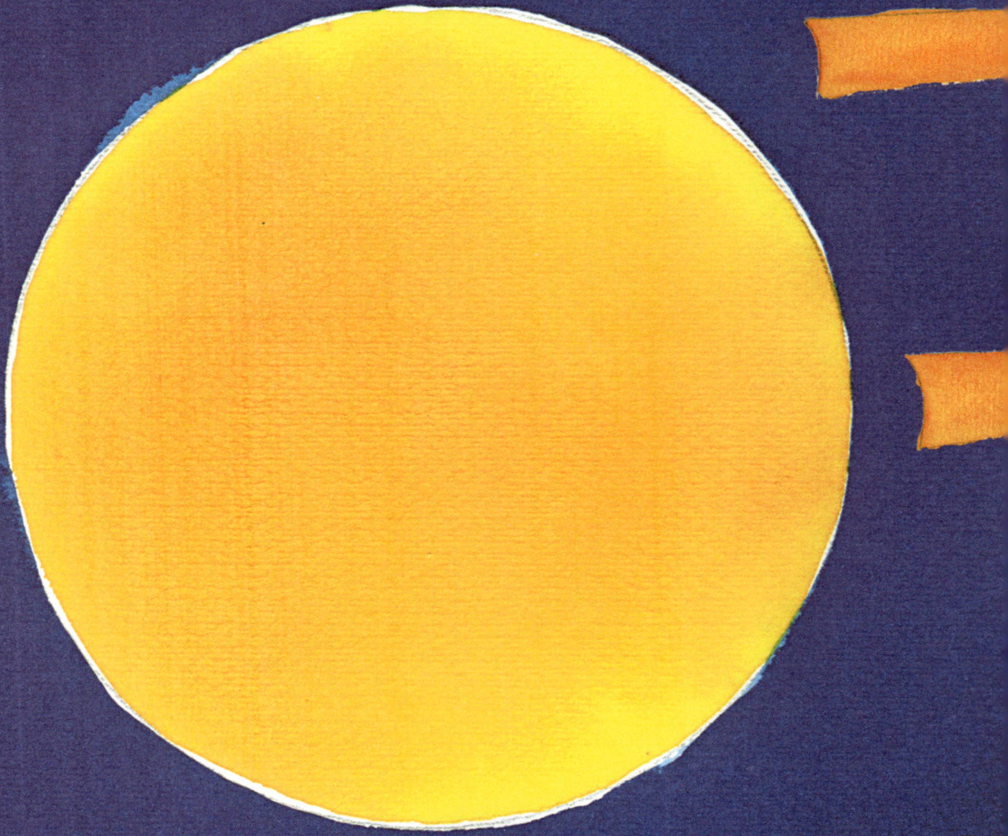

SUN

The Moon bounces light back from the Sun.

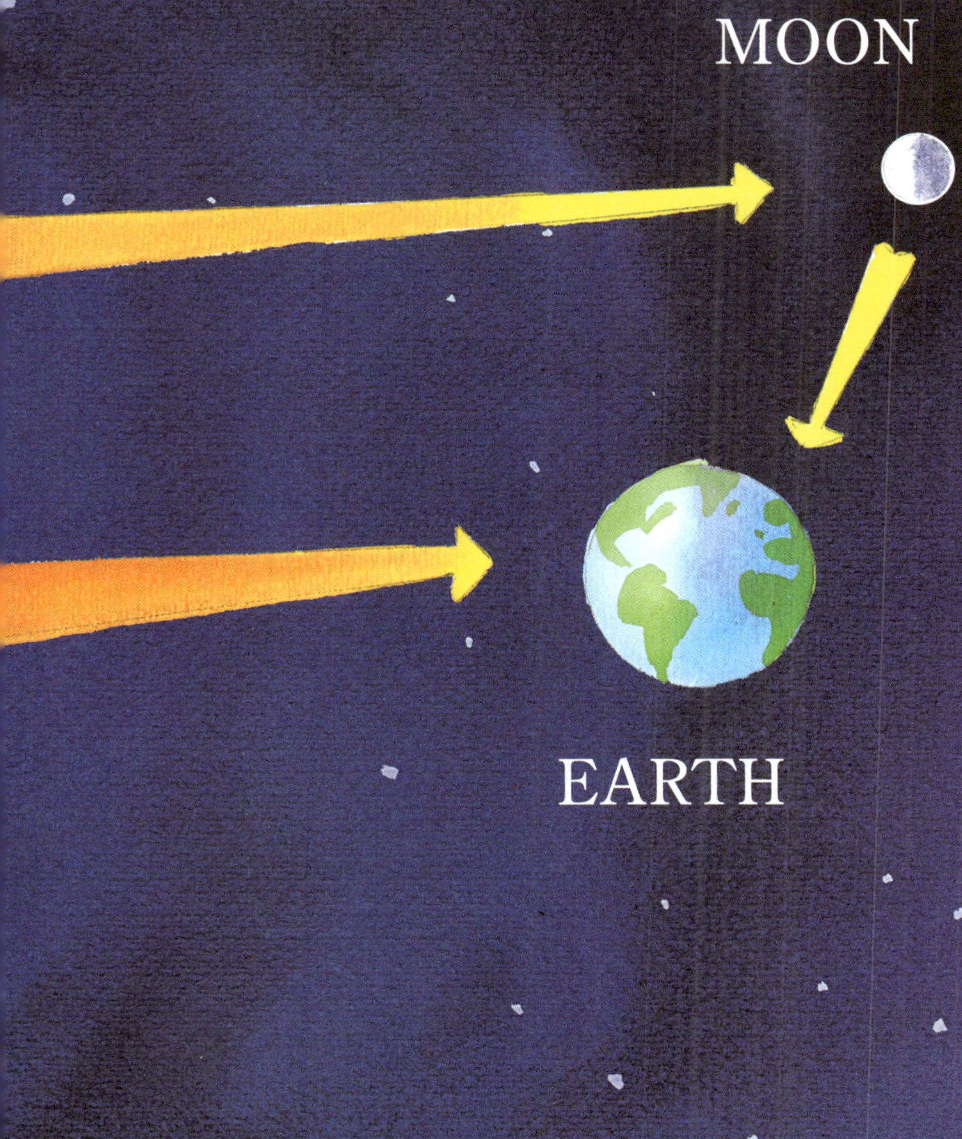

When the Moon passes behind the Earth, the Sun's light cannot reach it.

Then we have a lunar **eclipse**.

We never see the far side of the Moon.

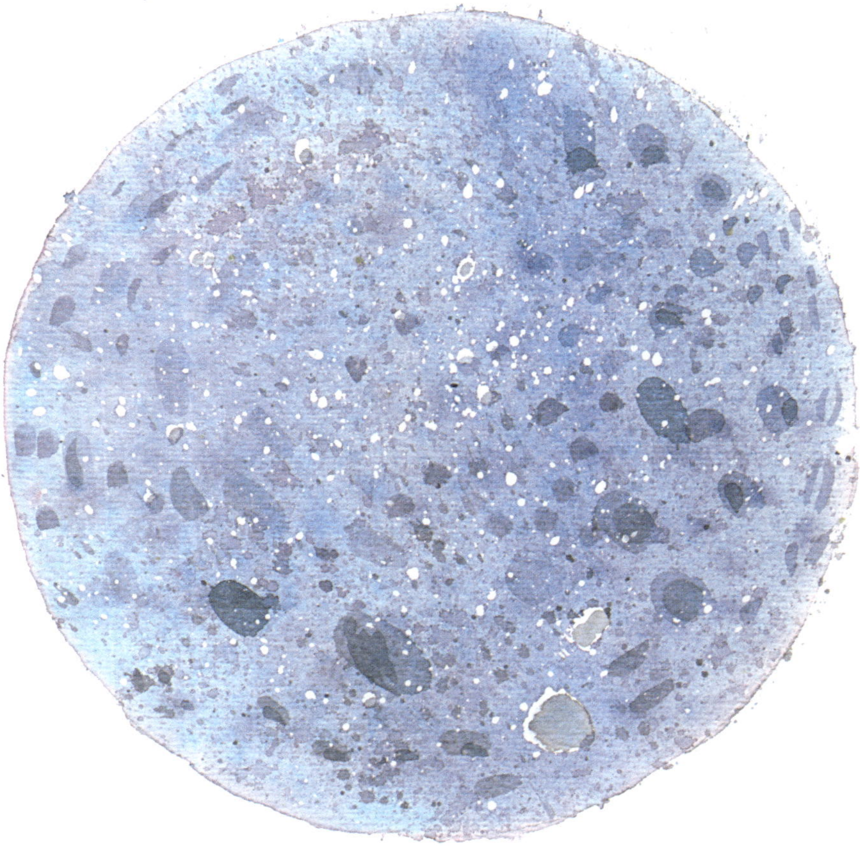

The Moon always keeps the same face toward Earth.

As the Moon circles Earth, the Sun lights up different parts of its face.

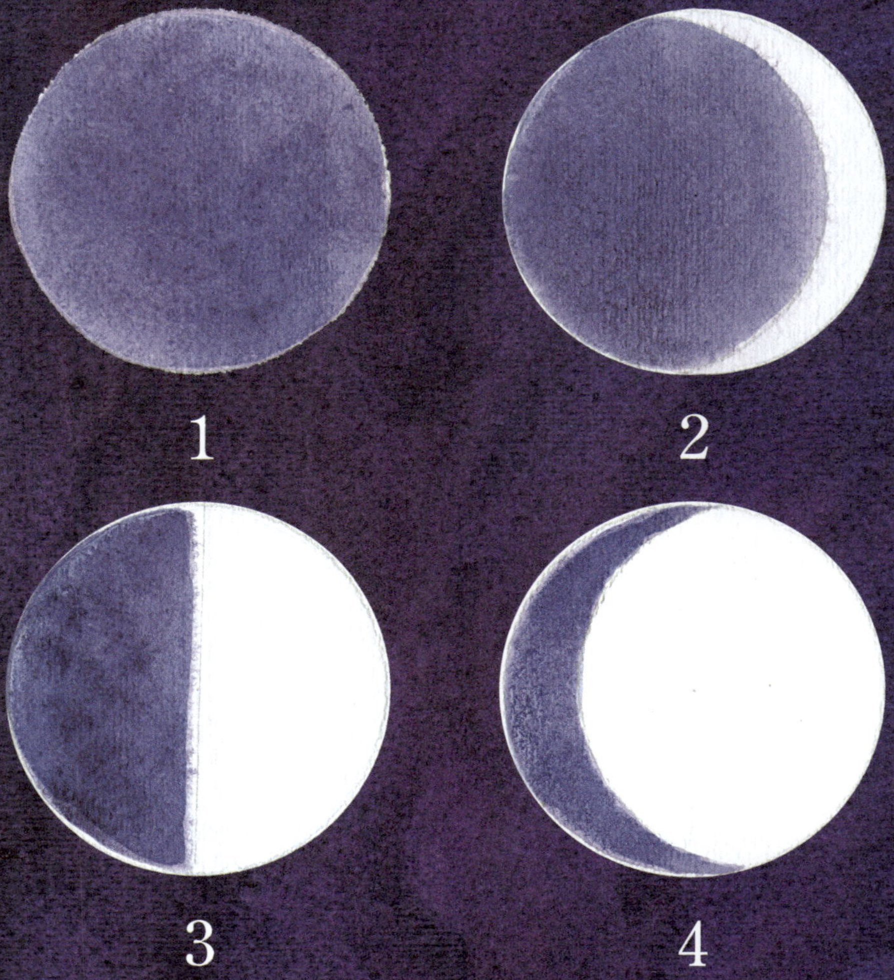

That is why the Moon's face keeps changing.

5

6

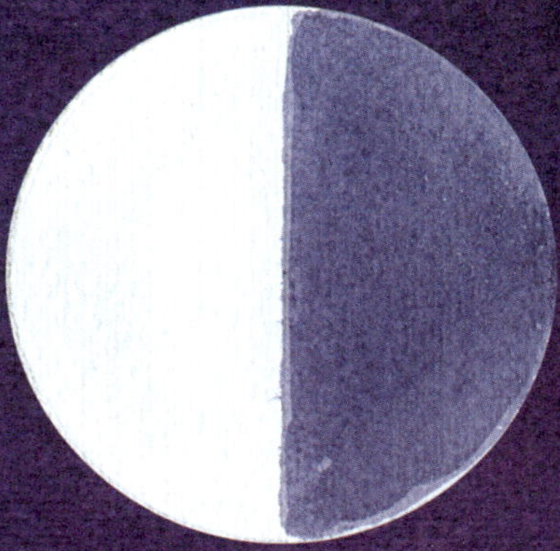

7

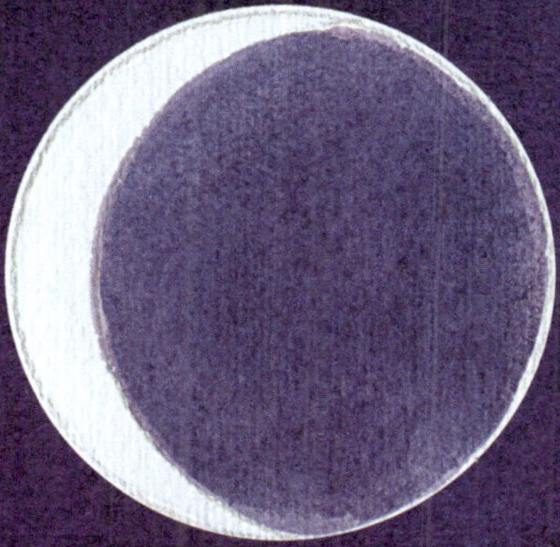

8

Have you ever seen
the man in the Moon?

That face was made long, long ago by **asteroids** striking the Moon.

Some see a woman in the Moon's craters.

Some see a rabbit

or even a frog!

In 1969 the United States
sent **astronauts** to the Moon.

Neil Armstrong became the first person to ever walk on the Moon.

The Moon has always been important to humans.

It brightens our nights.
It brightens our lives!

Interesting Facts

- ✦ Our Moon was formed around four and a half billion years ago.
- ✦ When the Moon appears to grow fuller, we call it a waxing Moon. When it appears to grow smaller, it is a waning Moon.
- ✦ The four main Moon phases are new Moon, first quarter Moon, full Moon, and third or last quarter Moon.
- ✦ There are over 200 moons in our solar system. Many of them orbit Saturn and Jupiter. Mars has two moons. Earth has only one.
- ✦ In 1959 the Soviets sent a spacecraft on a flyby past the Moon. They even took photos of the far side. That was the first time anyone saw what the far side looked like. Ten years later the United States sent *Apollo 11*, the first manned mission to land on the Moon.
- ✦ On July 20, 1969, Neil Armstrong stepped onto the Moon's surface and said, "That's one small step for a man, one giant leap for mankind."
- ✦ People used to wonder what the Moon was made of. Some made funny guesses like the Moon was made of blue cheese! Now that we have been there, we know it is made of rock and metal like our Earth.

OUR UNIVERSE

Mars

BY MARION DANE BAUER
ILLUSTRATED BY JOHN WALLACE

Ready-to-Read

Simon Spotlight
New York Amsterdam/Antwerp London
Toronto Sydney/Melbourne New Delhi

For my grandson, Brannon Bauer, with love —M. D. B.

To Simon and Betsy —J. G. W.

SIMON SPOTLIGHT
An imprint of Simon & Schuster Children's Publishing Division
1230 Avenue of the Americas, New York, New York 10020

This Simon Spotlight edition December 2025

Manufactured in China 0825 SDI

Glossary

- ✦ **astronaut** (say: A-struh-not): a person who goes into outer space. We refer to astronauts as "cosmonauts" when they are from Russia, "spationauts" when they are from France, and "taikonauts" when they are from China.
- ✦ **gravity** (say: GRA-vuh-tee): a pulling force that works across space. The bigger an object is, the more pull it has.
- ✦ **microbes** (say: MY-krohbs): life-forms so small that we can't see them.
- ✦ **oxygen** (say: AHK-sih-jun): a colorless, odorless gas. About 21 percent of the atmosphere on Earth is oxygen. Most organisms on Earth need oxygen to breathe.
- ✦ **poisonous** (say: POY-zuhn-us): something that causes harm when it touches the skin or enters the body.
- ✦ **scientists** (say: SIE-uhn-tists): people who observe and do research or experiments in a particular area of interest to better understand the world around us.
- ✦ **solar system** (say: SOH-luhr SIH-stum): the Sun together with the planets and their moons that orbit around it.

Note to readers: Some of these words may have more than one definition. The definitions above match how these words are used in this book.

Have you ever dreamed of
visiting Mars?

Flying to Mars in a spaceship would take six months or more. It would be a journey filled with surprises.

Even from far away
you would see why Mars
is called the Red Planet.

The red color comes
from iron dust in the air.

When you got to Mars,
our Sun would look small,
and the sky would be red.

But the sunset would be blue.

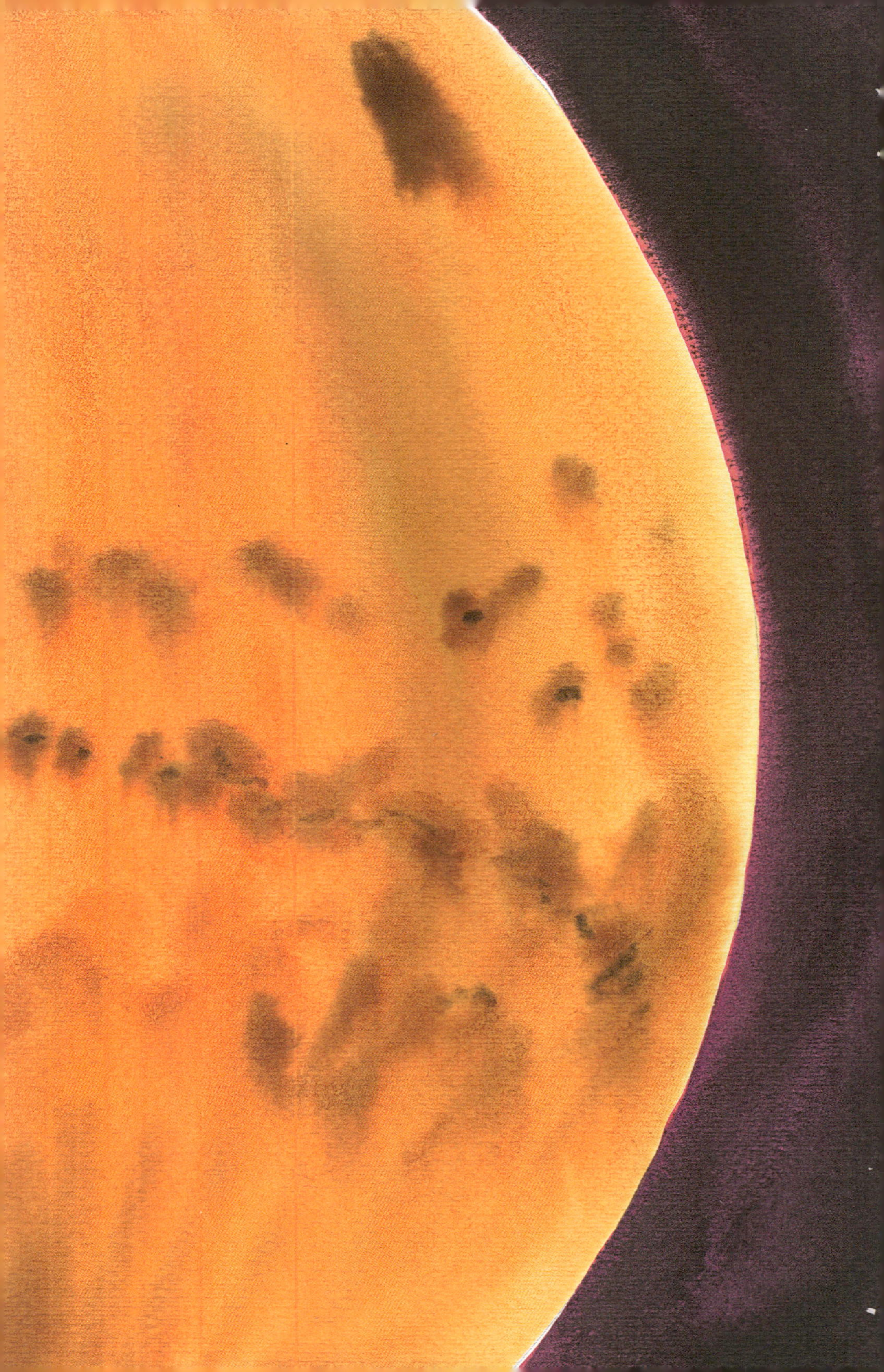

The night sky would hold two moons.

You could see the tallest volcano in our **solar system**, Olympus (say: uh-LIM-puhs) Mons.

Olympus Mons is 374 miles wide. But it rises so gently that it is almost flat.

You could see the canyon
Valles Marineris
(say: VA-luhs ma-ruh-NAIR-is).

In some places, the huge canyon is four miles deep. It is as wide as the entire United States.

You could jump almost three times higher on Mars than you can on Earth.

That is because Mars has less surface **gravity** than Earth.

But do not pack your
bags yet!

Mars is a harsh planet.

Mars has very little **oxygen** and almost no water. Even the ground may be **poisonous**.

We need oxygen and water to live.

And what about that wind?

Dust storms can last
for months!

Still, **scientists** love
to study Mars.

They hope to find signs of life there.

But they are looking for **microbes**,

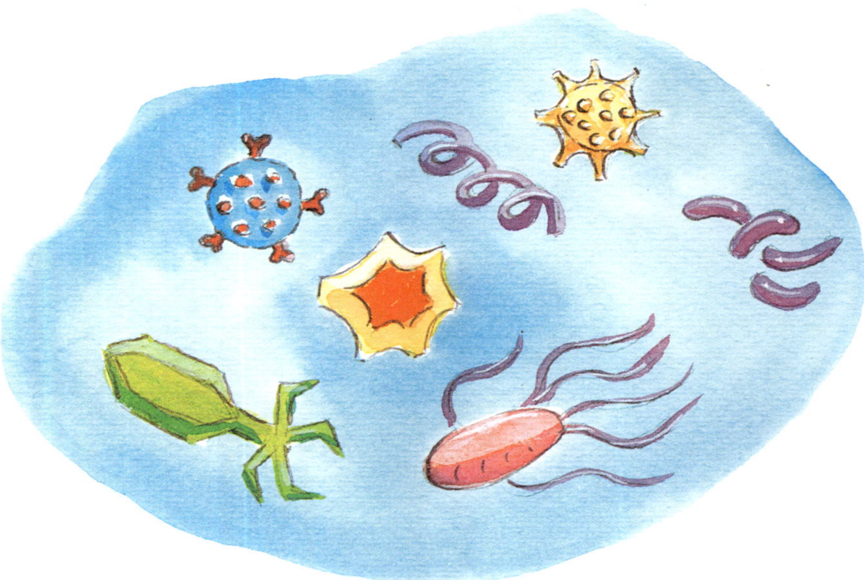

not aliens.

Many countries have sent spacecrafts to Mars.

Everyone wants to learn more about the Red Planet.

Maybe one day you will be the first **astronaut** to fly to Mars.

Or you might be a scientist
who discovers life there!

Interesting Facts

- ✦ Eight planets circle our Sun: Jupiter and Saturn are gas giants. Neptune and Uranus are ice giants. Mercury, Venus, Earth, and Mars are smaller and made of rock.
- ✦ Earth is the third planet from the Sun. Mars is the fourth.
- ✦ Mars is the planet most like ours. It is just a little more than half the size of Earth.
- ✦ The two moons of Mars are named Phobos and Deimos.
- ✦ Mars has frequent fierce storms. About once every three Martian years, a storm encircles the entire planet.
- ✦ The days on Mars are almost the same length as days on Earth, but the years are twice as long.
- ✦ The atmosphere on Mars is more than 95 percent carbon dioxide. Even the snow that falls near Mars's south pole is made of carbon dioxide.
- ✦ The average temperature of Mars is 80 degrees below zero Fahrenheit, and 63 degrees below zero Celsius.
- ✦ In 2021 the United States touched down on Mars. The parachute that gently lowered the space rover, *Perseverance*, to the surface had an orange-and-white design that carried the words "Dare Mighty Things" in code. The phrase is taken from a quote by former president Theodore Roosevelt.

Our Universe

The Milky Way

By Marion Dane Bauer

Illustrated by John Wallace

Ready-to-Read

Simon Spotlight
New York Amsterdam/Antwerp London
Toronto Sydney/Melbourne New Delhi

In memory of my brother, Willis Dane—M. D. B.

For Kelsey—J. W.

SIMON SPOTLIGHT
An imprint of Simon & Schuster Children's Publishing Division
1230 Avenue of the Americas, New York, New York 10020

This Simon Spotlight edition December 2025

Manufactured in China 0825 SDI

Glossary

- **asteroids** (say: A-stuh-royds): small, rocky bodies found in space that circle the Sun.
- **black hole**: a region in space with such a strong gravitational field that no light or matter can escape it.
- **comets** (say: KAH-mits): space objects made of ice that circle the Sun and often have long tails made of gas and dust.
- **disk**: a flat or thin object.
- **estimate** (say: ESS-tim-mate): to judge approximately.
- **galaxy** (say: GAH-luhk-see): a very large group of stars, planets, gas, dust, and other matter. Galaxies are found throughout the universe.
- **nebulae** (say: NEH-byuh-lee): clouds of gas and dust in outer space.

Note to readers: Some of these words may have more than one definition. The definitions above match how these words are used in this book.

Go far from city lights.
Look up at the night sky.
See that band of light?

That is the Milky Way.

The Milky Way is
a huge cluster of stars,
planets, gas, and dust
called a **galaxy**.

Every star you can see
with your bare eyes
is part of the Milky Way.

Our Sun is one
of hundreds of billions
of stars in our galaxy.

The Milky Way is a spiral galaxy.

From the side, it is
shaped like a **disk**.
From the top, it looks like
a spinning pinwheel.

The Milky Way
has spiral arms.

Our solar system lies
between two of those arms.

If our Sun was smaller
than a grain of sand,
the Milky Way would
span all of North America.

Our galaxy is that big!

Gas and dust make it difficult to see all that is there. But all we can see is beautiful.

There are ancient stars
and colorful **nebulae**.
And a very quiet **black hole**
in the center too.

Scientists **estimate** that there are about two trillion more galaxies just in the part of the universe they can see.

And no one knows
how many more
we have not yet seen.

You live in
an amazing universe.

It is filled with stars,
and planets,
and moons.

And **asteroids**,
and **comets**,
and dust,
and gas.

And lots, and lots,
and lots of space.

There is more empty space out there than anything else.

But down here on Earth
there is you.

And all that sky!

Interesting Facts

- ✦ Ancient Greeks told a story of the goddess Hera spraying milk across the sky. That is why we call our galaxy the Milky Way. In China that same band of stars is called the Silver River; in southern Africa it is called the Backbone of Night. It reminded hunter-gatherers in sub-Saharan Africa of campfire embers, while Polynesian sailors saw a cloud-eating shark.
- ✦ Galaxies come in many shapes and sizes: spiral, elliptical (egg shaped), or irregular. Some have only a few million stars. Some have over a trillion.
- ✦ Sometimes the Milky Way steals stars from other galaxies.
- ✦ Traveling at the speed of light, 186,000 miles per second, it would take 25,000 years to reach the center of the Milky Way from Earth.
- ✦ Our solar system orbits the center of the Milky Way once every 230 million years.
- ✦ Without a telescope, you can see about 6,000 stars from Earth. For every star you can see there are probably 20 million more you can't see because they are too far away or are blocked by clouds of cosmic dust.
- ✦ Scientists study other galaxies from the outside to learn about ours. They study the Milky Way from the inside to learn about other galaxies.

OUR UNIVERSE

Earth

BY MARION DANE BAUER
ILLUSTRATED BY JOHN WALLACE

Ready-to-Read

Simon Spotlight
New York Amsterdam/Antwerp London
Toronto Sydney/Melbourne New Delhi

For my grandson, Cullen Bauer-Trottier,
with love —M. D. B.

To Phoebe —J. G. W.

SIMON SPOTLIGHT
An imprint of Simon & Schuster Children's Publishing Division
1230 Avenue of the Americas, New York, New York 10020

This Simon Spotlight edition December 2025

Manufactured in China 0825 SDI

Glossary

- **amoebas** (say: ah-ME-bahs): tiny living things made of only one cell.
- **atmosphere** (say: at-MUH-sfir): the envelope of air surrounding a planet.
- **erupt**: to release or burst suddenly and violently against restraint.
- **Goldilocks zone** (say: GOAL-dee-locks zohn): in the story *The Three Bears*, Goldilocks found one porridge too hot, another too cold, and the third just right. A planet is in the "Goldilocks zone" when it is not too hot or too cold—just the right temperature for life.
- **scientists** (say: SIE-uhn-tists): people who observe and do research or experiments in a particular area of interest to better understand the world around us.
- **tilt**: to tip, lean, or slant.
- **water bears**: creatures so tiny they can only be seen through a microscope. They have four pairs of stout legs, and they usually live in water or damp moss. Their scientific name is "tardigrade." They are also called "moss piglets."
- **water vapor** (say: WAH-tuhr VAY-puhr): water as a gas instead of a liquid.

Note to readers: Some of these words may have more than one definition. The definitions above match the ways these words are used in this book.

Earth is a lucky planet.
It is just the right
distance from the Sun.

Not too hot.
Not too cold.
Scientists call this
the **Goldilocks zone**!

Each time Earth spins,

you wake up to a new day.

Each time Earth travels around the Sun,

you turn one year older.

Earth has a special **tilt** that gives us seasons.

The part that tips toward the Sun warms into summer.

The part that tips away cools into winter.

When Earth was born,
it was so hot, everything
was melted rock.

As it cooled, a crust formed.
Then volcanoes **erupted**
through the crust!

The volcanoes gave off **water vapor** and gases, forming our oceans and **atmosphere**.

Earth is the only planet we know that supports life.

Life on Earth can be as tiny as **amoebas** or **water bears**,

or as grand as redwood trees
or whales.

It can be as musical
as birds,

or as silent as fish.

Life on Earth can be
as sweet as a rose,

or as stinky as a skunk.

Or as stinky as
skunk cabbage!

You are part of
life on Earth too!

We humans are newcomers to this world,

but we live
all around the globe.

We live in forests,

beside oceans,

in cities,

and on farms.

We speak different languages and have different customs.

We wear different clothes

and live in different kinds of homes.

But we are all children of this Earth.

We must take care of our
home every day
of our lives.

Interesting Facts

- ✦ The Earth is more than four-and-a-half billion years old.
- ✦ The Sun is ninety-three million miles from our Earth. It takes eight minutes for light to travel from the Sun to us.
- ✦ Although we cannot feel the movement, we are zooming around the Sun at the amazing speed of eighteen-and-a-half miles per second!
- ✦ Many different factors make life as we know it possible on our planet. One is oxygen in our atmosphere. Another is the presence of water. And another is the temperature's being "just right." Earth's atmosphere gathers and holds the Sun's heat. Without our atmosphere, the temperature would be zero degrees all the time.

Climate Change

- ✦ Our planet is always changing, but humans are changing it faster than ever before. Burning fossil fuels and cutting down forests create big problems with our climate.
- ✦ Governments must work to solve these problems, but every person can help. We can plant trees. Trees store carbon and give back oxygen. We can use water with care. All life needs water. We can recycle to keep trash from our oceans and our land. And we can learn more about the climate crisis. All of these actions help care for the planet we call home.

OUR UNIVERSE

THE Night Sky

BY MARION DANE BAUER
ILLUSTRATED BY JOHN WALLACE

Ready-to-Read

Simon Spotlight
New York Amsterdam/Antwerp London
Toronto Sydney/Melbourne New Delhi

For Eugenie Doyle —M. D. B.

To the children of Vatsalya —J. W.

SIMON SPOTLIGHT
An imprint of Simon & Schuster Children's Publishing Division
1230 Avenue of the Americas, New York, New York 10020

This Simon Spotlight edition December 2025

Manufactured in China 0825 SDI

Glossary

- **atmosphere** (say: AT-muh-sfeer): the envelope of gases surrounding Earth.
- **constellations** (say: kon-stuh-LAY-shuhns): groups of stars forming recognizable patterns. Different people at different times in history have used their own favorite stories to find images in the stars.
- **meteors** (say: MEE-tee-ors): dust or rocks from outer space that burn when they enter Earth's atmosphere, appearing to us as streaks of light.
- **northern lights** (aurora borealis) (say: uh-RORE-uh bore-ee-A-luss): a display of colorful lights in the sky seen mostly in the far north. The lights are caused by solar wind. They occur near the South Pole, too, and then are called southern lights (aurora australis).
- **Perseid meteor shower** (say: PUR-see-ud MEE-tee-or SHAU-er): a heavier-than-usual display of meteors that appears in mid-August. The name comes from the fact that the meteors seem to radiate from a point in a constellation known as Perseus.
- **telescope** (say: TEH-luh-skohp): an instrument designed to make distant objects appear nearer.

Note to readers: Some of these words may have more than one definition. The definitions above match how these words are used in this book.

Did you know that stars shine day and night?

We do not see stars
in the daytime
because the star
closest to us, our sun,
outshines them all.

To see the night sky
in all its glory,
leave city lights behind.

Wait for your eyes
to get used to the dark.
Then look up.
Wow!

On most nights,
you can see our moon first.
Because it is so close,
it seems larger
than anything else.

The moon's face
changes every night.
Sometimes it is round.

Sometimes it is
just a sliver.

Then there are all
those twinkling stars.

They twinkle because their light bounces and bumps through our **atmosphere** to reach us.

Humans have always made connect-the-dots pictures with the stars.

We call those
pictures **constellations**.

The ancient Greeks
imagined the hunter Orion
in this group of stars.

In the same stars,
the Navajo saw the
First Slender One,
a warrior protecting
his people.

Planets are closer
than stars, so they
do not twinkle.
They look like
flat disks of light.

Mercury, Venus,
Mars, Jupiter,
and Saturn can all be
seen without a **telescope**.

Have you ever seen
a falling star?

Falling stars are
not really stars.
They are **meteors**.

Meteors are made up of rocks from outer space.

Most burn up before
they reach the ground.
But if they do land,
they are called meteorites.

In August during the
Perseid meteor shower,
you might see up to
one hundred meteors
in an hour.

Many stories are told about the **northern lights**. In China people saw a battle between dragons in those lights.

In Finland the lights are
foxes brushing snowflakes
into the sky
with their tails.

Whatever story they tell,
these dancing lights
are spectacular!

Do you want to glimpse
our fascinating universe?
Just look at the night sky.

Wow!

Interesting Facts

- About nine thousand stars are visible to the bare eye, but only half are visible from one place. That's because half of Earth is always in sunlight, which means that all the stars aren't visible at the same time.
- Ancient sailors navigated by measuring the position of certain stars to the horizon. Modern sailors and even airplane pilots can navigate by the stars too.
- The North Star stands almost directly over the North Pole, so it can be used to find north. It holds nearly still in the sky while all the other stars appear to move around it.
- The Big Dipper is a favorite image in the sky. It is called an asterism, not a constellation, because it is part of a bigger constellation, Ursa Major (Great Bear).
- Big telescopes on the ground use lasers and mirrors to take the twinkle out of starlight so astronomers can see the stars more clearly.
- In 1990 the United States guided a powerful telescope, Hubble, into orbit 332 miles above Earth's surface. For more than thirty years Hubble has sent back images that have taught us much about our universe.
- In 2021 the James Webb Space Telescope was launched into orbit. It traveled a million miles from Earth. The Webb is one hundred times more powerful than the Hubble and can see much farther into space, revealing a universe we have only been able to imagine before now.